My Awesome DINOSAUR BOOK

make believe ideas

DINOSAURS

Dinosaurs were animals that lived over 66 million years ago. The word *dinosaur* means "terrible lizard."

Tyrannosaurus rex

Deinonychus

Diplodocus

Dinosaurs were **reptiles.** They hatched from **eggs.**

Parasauroiophus

Pachycephalosaurus

TYRANNOSAURUS REX

(tye-RAN-oh-SORE-us rex)

T. rex was one of the fiercest dinosaurs to ever walk the earth.

HOW BIG?

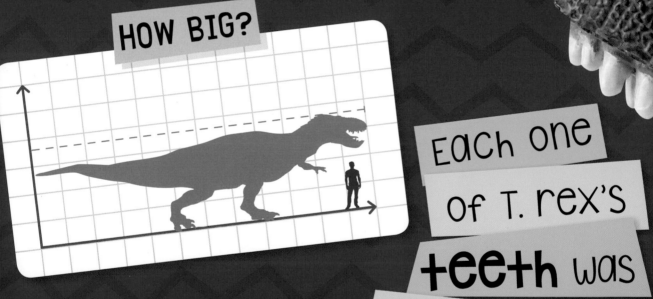

Each one of T. rex's **teeth** was the size of a **banana!**

Want some tea, REX?

STEGOSAURUS

(STEG-oh-SORE-us)

Stegosaurus was as big as a bus, but its brain was as small as a walnut!

Don't leave me in the rain, I'll Stegosau-**RUST**!

Large **spikes** helped Stegosaurus to **defend** itself.

HOW BIG?

TRICERATOPS

(tri-SERR-ah-tops)

Triceratops had horns that were as long as hockey sticks.

horn →

HOW BIG?

I NEVER give up. I'm a TRY-TRY-TRICERATOPS!

In a fight, Triceratops would **run** at other dinosaurs and **headbutt** them!

VELOCIRAPTOR

(vel-OSS-ee-rap-tor)

Velociraptor was very fierce, but it was only the size of a turkey!

Want to know my FAVORITE store? The DINO-STORE!

HOW BIG?

velociraptor was one of the **smartest** dinosaurs.

BRACHIOSAURUS

(BRACK-ee-oh-SORE-us)

With its long neck and front legs, Brachiosaurus stood like a giraffe, but three times taller.

HOW BIG?

I'm HEAD and SHOULDERS above the rest!

one BRACHIOSAURUS could **weigh** as much as **six** African elephants!

SPINOSAURUS

(SPINE-oh-SORE-us)

Spinosaurus had a spiny sail on its back and was a huge meat-eater!

JUST **one** of spinosaurus' **spines** was around **twice** your **height!**

I spy a
SPY-nosaurus ...

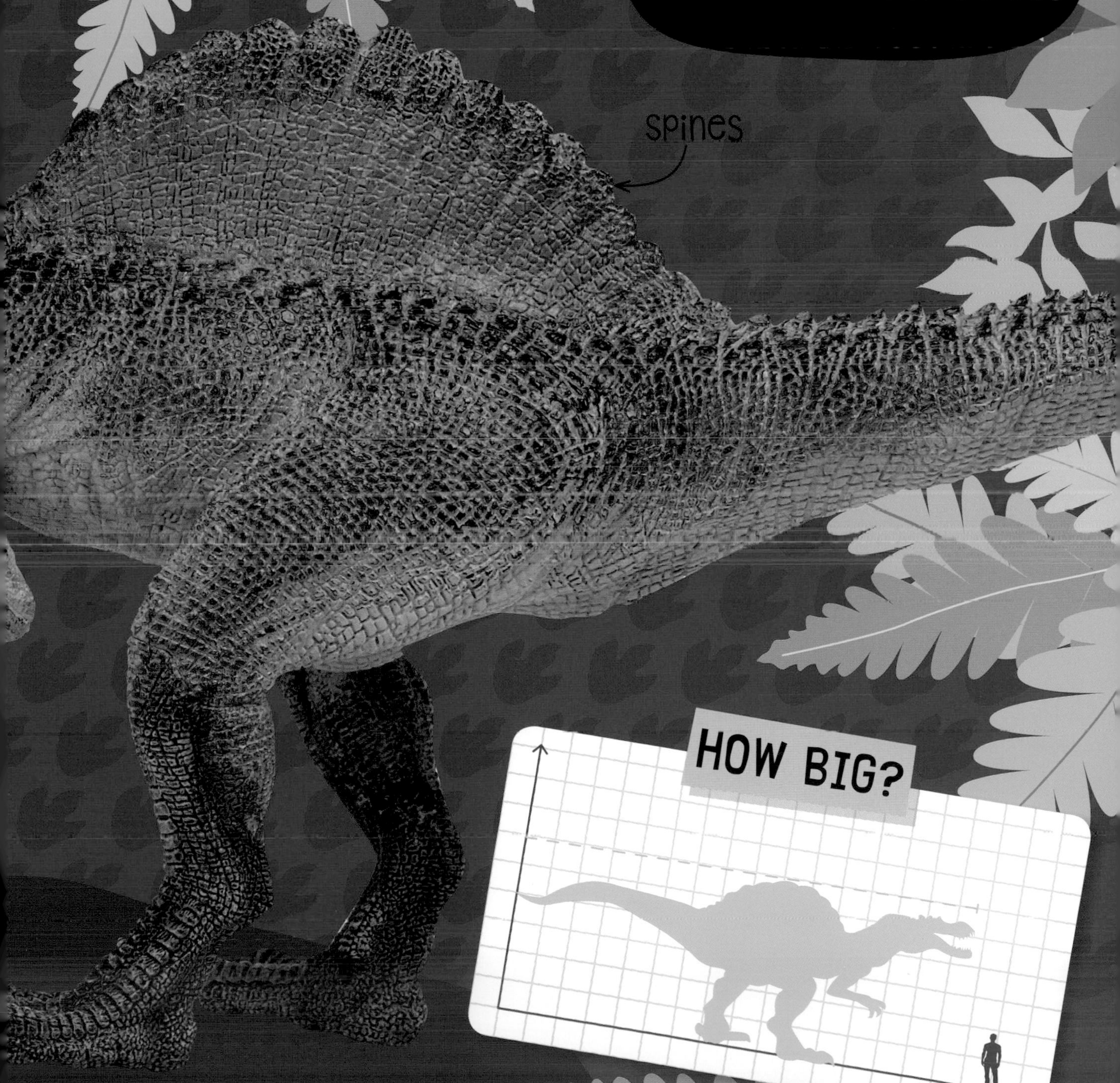

HOW BIG?

PARASAUROLOPHUS

(pa-ra-SORE-OH-lo-fus)

Parasaurolophus was a strange-looking dinosaur with a long, bony crest on its head.

HOW BIG?

crest

Parasaurolophus' **crest** may have been used to make **loud trumpet** sounds!

What's louder than ONE Parasaurolophus?

TWO Parasaurolophus!

DEINONYCHUS

(die-NON-i-kus)

Deinonychus was super-fast and had feathers like a bird.

HOW BIG?

I'm **CLAW**-some!

Deinonychus means "terrible claw." It was named after its huge claws!

claw

ANKYLOSAURUS

(AN-kee-lo-SORE-us)

Ankylosaurus was as big as a tank and had heavily armored skin.

Want to join my CLUB?

club tail

ANKYLOSAURUS'
POWERFUL

club tail

could probably

break the leg

of a T. rex!

HOW BIG?

LAMBEOSAURUS

(LAM-bee-oh-SORE-us)

Lambeosaurus was named after Lawrence Lambe, the man who discovered it.

HOW BIG?

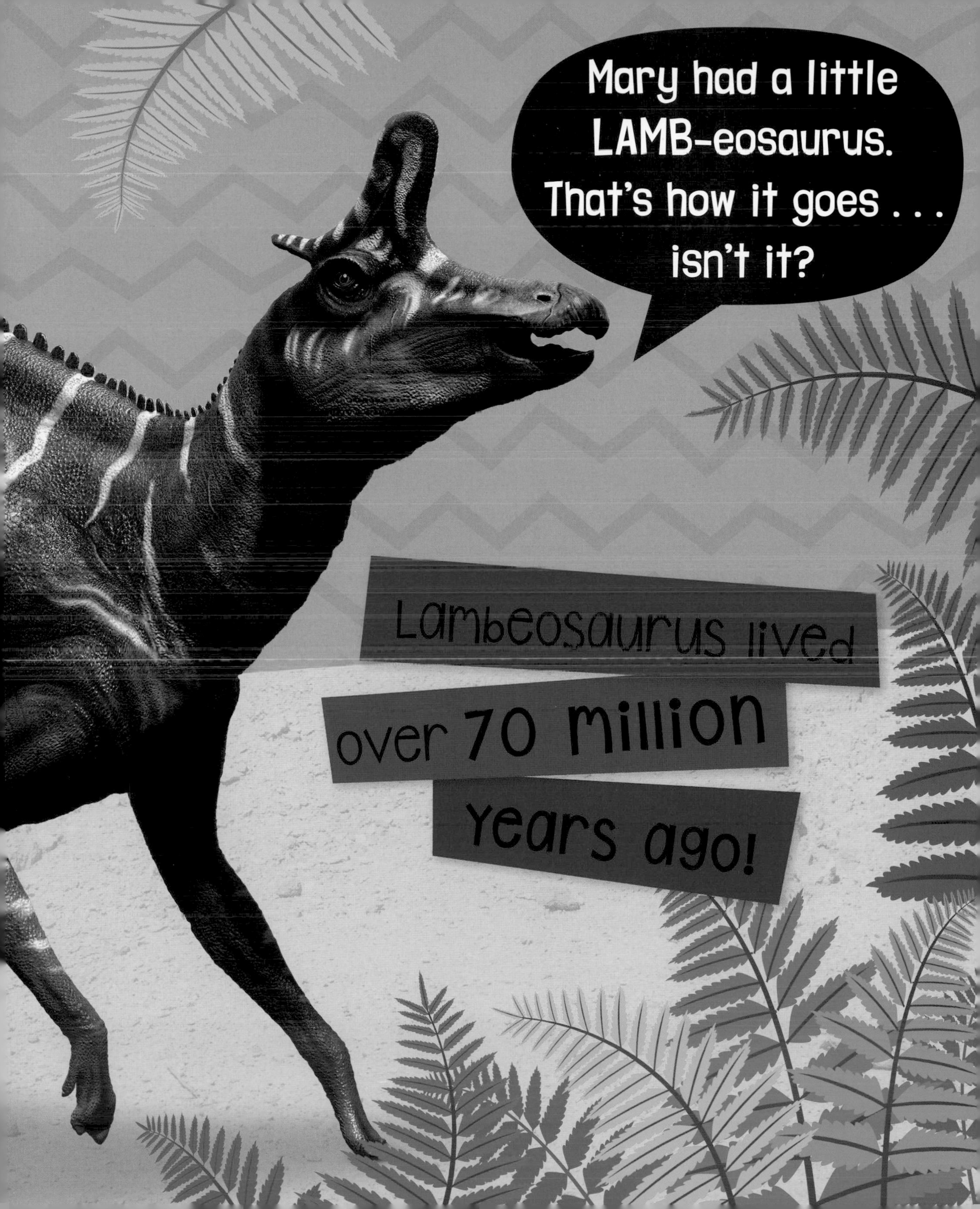

Lambeosaurus lived over 70 million years ago!

PACHYCEPHALOSAURUS

(pack-ee-SEF-ah-lo-SORE-us)

Pachycephalosaurus had a large dome of bone on its head, which it used to headbutt rivals.

HOW BIG?

I'm such a BONEHEAD!

Just like humans, pachycephalosaurus had ten fingers.

IGUANODON

(ig-WAN-oh-don)

The peaceful plant-eater Iguanodon
was one of the first dinosaurs
to ever be named.

HOW BIG?

Give me a THUMBS-UP!

Iguanodon used their **thumbs** to rip **leaves** off trees.

thumb

ALLOSAURUS

(AL-oh-SORE-us)

Allosaurus was a meat-eater who lived alongside Diplodocus and Stegosaurus.

HOW BIG?

Allosaurus had around

70 teeth!

SMILE and say, "HALLO-saurus!"

DID YOU KNOW?

All dinosaurs lived on land. Animals that flew or lived in the ocean were not dinosaurs.

Elasmosaurus had one of the longest necks of any creature that has ever lived.

These dinosaur jokes are PTERRIBLE!
Hey! WATER you up to?
Pterodactylus means
"Winged flyer!"
Eek! Do-you-think-he-saurus?